Magical Night

by Kristi McGee
illustrated by Maurice J. Manning

Harcourt
SCHOOL PUBLISHERS

Printed in Mexico

ISBN 10: 0-15-351670-4
ISBN 13: 978-0-15-351670-2

Ordering Options
ISBN 10: 0-15-351215-6 (Grade 5 Advanced Collection)
ISBN 13: 978-0-15-351215-5 (Grade 5 Advanced Collection)
ISBN 10: 0-15-358153-0 (package of 5)
ISBN 13: 978-0-15-358153-3 (package of 5)

4 5 6 7 8 9 10   126   12 11 10 09 08

"This is my worst nightmare! I don't think I can do it!" I cried to my mom. Earlier that day, my teacher had announced that there would be no class music program this year. Instead, we would be having a talent show. That way, she had said, *everyone* would get time in the limelight. The problem is I do NOT want the time.

My hand shot into the air. "Ms. Grace," I said with a quiver in my voice, "I don't like the spotlight." My classmates laughed. I was dead serious. I had a downright phobia about doing anything in front of people, let alone performing in a talent show. I pleaded with Ms. Grace, but it didn't matter what I said to her. She was not changing her mind.

"Tavon," she said, "everyone has a talent. It's your job to share that talent with the whole community." My stomach jumped into my throat. It rolled over once. Then it flopped down to my ankles.

I told Mom what Ms. Grace had said. Can you believe this? Mom agreed! Even she didn't understand. It is really hard for me to raise my hand in class. It is hard for me to say my name in front of a group. It is even hard for me to talk to my friends sometimes. Now they want me to share my talent. I am supposed to share it with not just my class, but the whole school and their parents. My talent is being quiet! I am best at hiding from people!

Of course, I didn't tell Mom any of this. I figured I had to go it alone. How was I going to get out of performing? How could I stand up in front of an audience and perform anything? The thought of it made me want to cry. I needed to be creative. Maybe I could get sick on the day of the show. I immediately vetoed that idea. Mom would know I was faking. "There's nothing I can do about it now," I thought.

I changed into my pajamas and tried to sleep. My dreams were riddled with it being my turn to take the stage at the talent show. I barely slept a wink.

The next day, all I heard was talk of the talent show. The drama club worked on writing a skit from *Gulliver's Travels.* I heard someone say, "Hey, Tavon, do you want to be a Lilliputian?"

The people from Lilliput are tiny. The part wouldn't require that I say much, and the group needed someone small. Since I am one of the smallest kids in my class, it seemed like a perfect fit.

Then I heard Jay say, "I think we should act out the part of the Yahoos instead." The group agreed. I didn't think I would make a particularly convincing big bully, so I politely bowed out of the play.

I was back where I began, with no idea what to do and even less time to think about it.

As all my classmates were preparing and practicing their talents, I was without a clue as to what to do. However, even at this point, I was not discouraged. I continued to brainstorm ideas that would either showcase a talent I had that did not involve speaking, or would convince Ms. Grace that I did not need to participate in the talent show.

In fact, I was so convinced that I could come up with a great idea that would solve my problem that even as Ms. Grace reviewed the rules for punctuation, I was busy devising a plan for the talent show. I had already ruled out being sick. What if I told Ms. Grace I was going on vacation that week? No. I had already told Mom about the show. Besides, I would have to find somewhere to go all week. I couldn't come to school. What if I said there was an invasion of distant relatives in my house, so I had no time to prepare for the show? I doubted Ms. Grace would be swayed by that lie.

"Tavon? Tavon? Are you listening?" Ms. Grace jarred me from my daydream.

"Sorry. What was the question?" I asked.

"There was no question, Tavon," the teacher said. "I was just commending you on your excellent story." There went my stomach again—up, over, down. I felt sick. I must have known what was coming next.

"Will you please come up and read it to the class, Tavon?" she asked.

Did I mention I'm shy? I am painfully, horribly, sickly shy. I almost burst into tears. Luckily, Ms. Grace took pity on me. "Maybe I will just read it," she said mercifully. I nodded at her and smiled.

Ms. Grace started reading aloud. At first, I tried to keep my head up, but everyone was looking at me. Slowly, as if by itself, my head sunk down onto my desk. Then my arms covered my head. I couldn't look. I couldn't think. I could barely hear. It seemed like forever, and then I heard clapping.

The girl beside me leaned over and said, "You can look now," while the boy behind me gave me a "nice job" pat on my back.

After class ended, I went to retrieve my story. Ms. Grace said, "I really think you should consider reading this for the talent show." My eyes glazed over with tears. "Maybe we could work something out where you read offstage. That way you wouldn't have to look at the audience." Quite frankly, that sounded scary, too. It sounded a lot better than reading it onstage, though.

I quietly said, "Thank you, Ms. Grace." I knew she was trying to be nice.

Now I knew I wasn't going to get out of it, so I surrendered and decided I'd have to prepare for it. I started reading. I read that story what seemed like a million times. I stood in front of the mirror to read. I sat in my chair and read. I recorded my reading on tape. I read to my mom, my dad, and my neighbor, Mr. Elroy. By the time I was done practicing, I practically knew the story by heart. I still trembled at the thought of reading it with all those people listening. It didn't matter that I wouldn't see them.

Two weeks before the talent show was our first official rehearsal. We had three rehearsals to try to get the show together. I don't know if it was the best or worst thing, but I was chosen to go last. Part of me wished I were first. I wanted to just get it over with! The paper shook so much in my hands that I could barely make out the words. That was still an hour before I was supposed to read! "I'll never get through this," I thought. Just then, something magical happened.

Ms. Grace entered the auditorium and said, "Kids, I have some bad news. Jinny took a spill while she was ice-skating. She's injured her leg and won't be able to do the show. Unfortunately, Mae Lin, that means you will have to find a new assistant for your magic show."

Now you might think I am mean for calling that magical. You just wait and see.

Mae Lin started to cry. "What am I going to do? My magic show won't work without Jinny! We've been practicing for days! She knew exactly what to do! Who else is small enough to fit through that little, tiny trapdoor?" All of a sudden, I felt about thirty pairs of eyes boring into me.

"Maybe Tavon can help," Ms. Grace suggested.

At first, I thought this was a horrible idea. There was no way I was going to do it. Mae Lin sized me up. "I think you'll do," she said. She stood almost a foot taller than me. She sounded as if her mind was made up.

"I ... I ... I ... " I sputtered.

"Come with me, Tavon," Mae Lin commanded. She was a no-nonsense kind of person.

She took me backstage to show me the props for the
tricks. She said, "This job will be perfect for you." She opened
a large, black box just big enough for a person. It had several
compartments. She described what each one held and did.
All I had to do was stand inside the box. I could even keep my
eyes closed. I needed to quickly climb through the trapdoor at
the back after she closed me in. Then she turned the
box around three times and yelled some magic word like
abracadabra or *alakazaam*. Oh, yeah, and first I had to stick
a stuffed dog in the bottom of the box to replace me. Then I
had to put a stuffed rabbit in to replace the dog. It was magic!
I had the perfect behind-the-scenes job. As I said before, I am
good at hiding. I am even better at disappearing.

Soon the night of the show was upon us. Mae Lin's magic act was next to last. I helped her wheel the box out onstage and quickly climbed inside it. Then Mae Lin gave her whole speech about how I would disappear and a rabbit would appear. She closed the door and spun the box around. I scrambled out the trapdoor and grabbed the stuffed dog. I quickly put it in the box where I had been. Mae Lin opened the box to stun the audience with the ... rabbit?

"Oops!" Mae Lin exclaimed, pretending to be surprised. She bent over to give the dog a pet. "This dog of mine, you never know when it will show up." The audience roared. "Let's try again. I know I can get the rabbit." Mae Lin spun the box around again. Now I had to quickly exchange the dog for the rabbit. No one ever said that would be easy! The audience went wild when the rabbit appeared.

Everyone was clapping. I felt really proud of the work I did. Maybe big crowds weren't that bad after all. Then everything settled down. I didn't know who was going to be last now that I wasn't reading my story. Suddenly, I saw Jinny being wheeled onstage. She had a cast from her hip to her toe, sticking straight out from the wheelchair. She had a paper on her lap. As Ms. Grace turned her to face the audience, Jinny smiled as she pushed her wispy bangs out of her eyes.

"I guess I'm not as good an ice skater as I am a ballet dancer." The audience expressed their sympathy. Then Jinny said, "At first, I was going to be in Mae Lin's magic act but couldn't for obvious reasons. Instead, Ms. Grace asked me to take the place of the person who stood in for me. Now I will read his story. It is called "Fly, Fly Away," and it is by the famous, disappearing Tavon Jones."

I couldn't believe my ears. Jinny started reading. I could see the audience members from the wings of the stage. They were paying attention. I heard them laugh. I think I even saw one person shed a tear. My mom wore a smile from ear to ear. My dad had that serious look of approval on his face.

Jinny finished the story to thundering applause. I knew that applause was for me—for a story I wrote all by myself. I felt my stomach do something funny, but this time it wasn't so bad. I was feeling excited, and I was feeling really good about myself. All these people really liked what I had written.

Then came the curtain call. One by one, students' names were called to go out and take a bow. Ms. Grace called Mae Lin's name and then Jinny's. Finally, she called me. I had to walk out there, all by myself, in front of the whole crowd. I discovered that I wasn't afraid anymore—at least not as afraid as I would have been before. I walked right out on center stage and took a big bow as the audience continued to clap. When I stood up, I had a beaming smile on my face.

The night of the talent show was the beginning of my getting over my fear of appearing in front of people. That night was truly magical.

Think Critically

1. Why do you think Tavon's mother does not help him to get out of the talent show?

2. What is the main idea of the story?

3. What are three important details that led up to Tavon changing his mind about performing in front of people?

4. How would you feel if you had to perform in a talent show? What would you do for the show?

5. How has the author organized the information in this story?

Science

Flying Animals Tavon's story was called "Fly, Fly Away." Choose an animal that can fly. Take notes and write a short report on the animal, using some of the information you found. You may wish to call your report "Fly, Fly Away."

 School-Home Connection Tell a family member about this story. Share your feelings with one another about performing in front of people.

Word Count: 2,073